South Australia
A Pictorial

AXIOM

Produced entirely in South Australia.

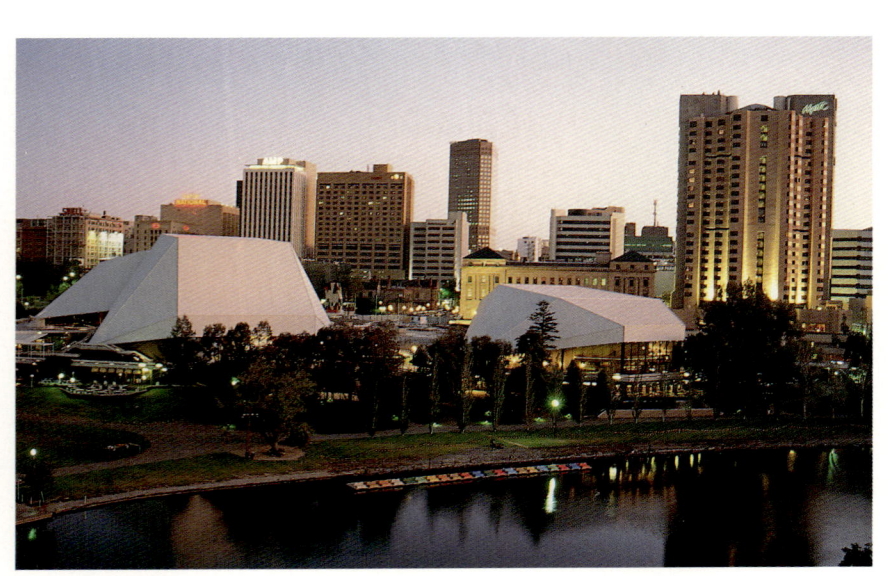

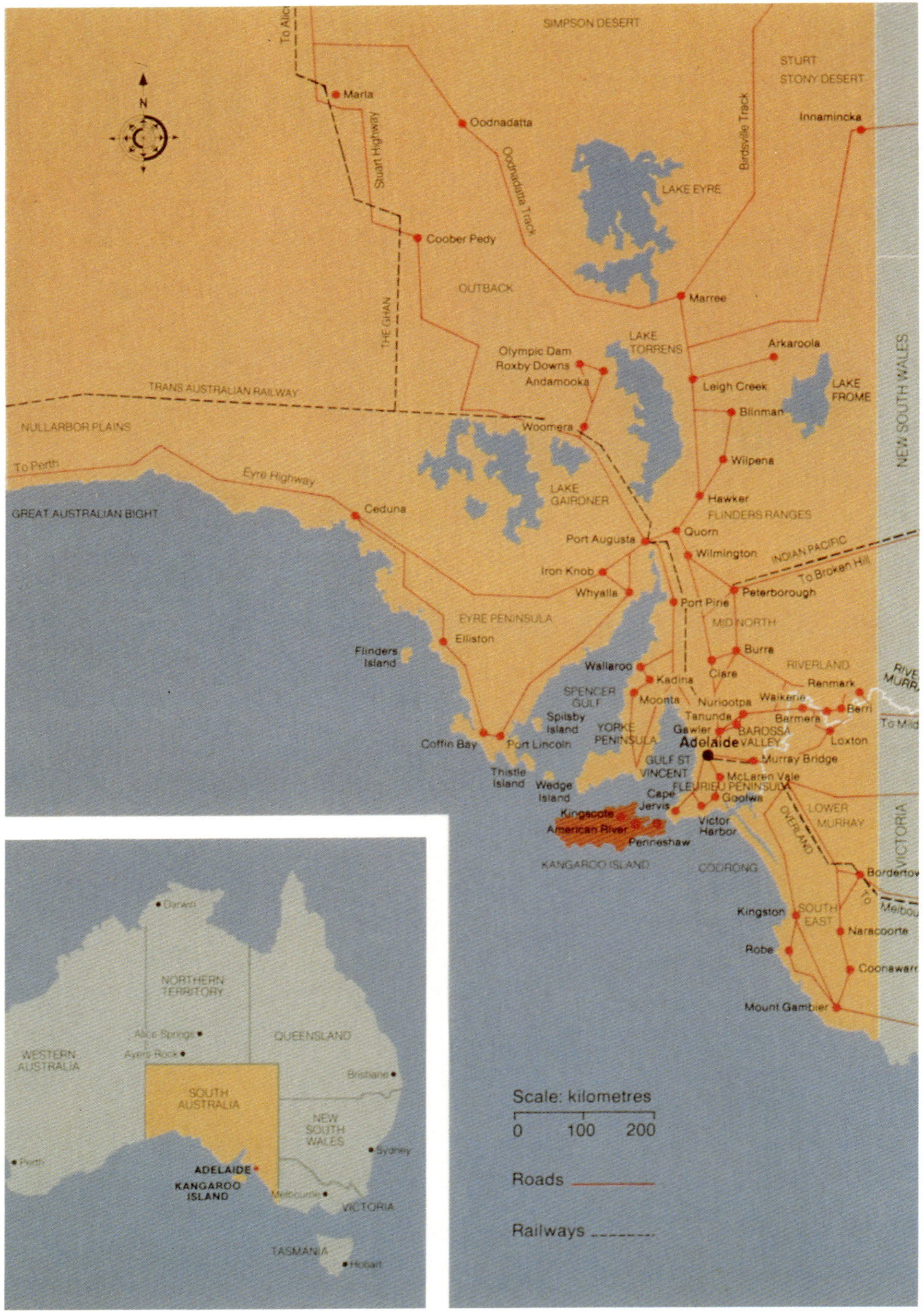

SIMPSON DESERT
STURT STONY DESERT
Marla
Oodnadatta
Stuart Highway
Oodnadatta Track
Birdsville Track
Innamincka
LAKE EYRE
Coober Pedy
OUTBACK
THE GHAN
Marree
LAKE TORRENS
Olympic Dam
Roxby Downs
Andamooka
Arkaroola
Leigh Creek
LAKE FROME
TRANS AUSTRALIAN RAILWAY
Blinman
NULLARBOR PLAINS
Woomera
Wilpena
To Perth
Eyre Highway
LAKE GAIRDNER
Hawker
FLINDERS RANGES
GREAT AUSTRALIAN BIGHT
Ceduna
Port Augusta
Quorn
Wilmington
INDIAN PACIFIC
To Broken Hill
Iron Knob
Whyalla
Port Pirie
Peterborough
EYRE PENINSULA
MID NORTH
Elliston
Burra
Flinders Island
RIVERLAND
Wallaroo
Kadina
Clare
Renmark
SPENCER GULF
Moonta
Nuriootpa
Waikerie
Tanunda
Barmera
Berri
Spilsby Island
YORKE PENINSULA
Gawler
BAROSSA VALLEY
Loxton
Coffin Bay
Port Lincoln
Adelaide
Murray Bridge
GULF ST VINCENT
Thistle Island
Wedge Island
McLaren Vale
FLEURIEU PENINSULA
Cape Jervis
Goolwa
LOWER MURRAY
Kingscote
American River
Victor Harbor
Penneshaw
KANGAROO ISLAND
COORONG
NEW SOUTH WALES
VICTORIA
Bordertown
Kingston
SOUTH EAST
Naracoorte
Robe
Mount Gambier
Scale: kilometres
0
100
200
Roads
Railways
Darwin
NORTHERN TERRITORY
QUEENSLAND
WESTERN AUSTRALIA
Alice Springs
Ayers Rock
Brisbane
SOUTH AUSTRALIA
NEW SOUTH WALES
Perth
Sydney
ADELAIDE
KANGAROO ISLAND
Melbourne
VICTORIA
TASMANIA
Hobart

The publisher wishes to thank
the following individuals and organisations.

Mortlock Library for the 'Early Settlement' photographs.
Tourism South Australia,
in particular Bob Nichols and Nancye Fowler.
David Sinclair.
Pamela Attwood.
Don McLennan.
Stephen Sanders.
Katharine Stafford.
Paul Stratton.

Proudly printed in South Australia by
Stock Journal Printing

ISBN O 947338 22 5

Copyright © Axiom 1991
This book is copyright. Apart from any fair
dealing for the purpose of private study,
research, criticism or review, as permitted
under the Copyright Act, no part may be
reproduced by any process without written
permission.
Enquiries should be made to the publisher.

Axiom
Adelaide
South Australia

CONTENTS

This is South Australia	4
Arts and Entertainment	5
Sport and Recreation	6
Business and Technology	7
Early Settlement	8
Adelaide	18
Adelaide Hills	26
Wine Growing Regions	28
Fleurieu Peninsula	32
Riverland	34
South East	36
Yorke Peninsula	38
Eyre Peninsula	40
Flinders Ranges	42
Mid North	46
Far North	48
Kangaroo Island	50
Seasonal Guide	52

This is South Australia

—with its pleasant, easy-going climate and pleasures to tempt every visitor: from the sophistication and excitement of the Adelaide Casino to peaceful bed-and-breakfast escapes in little country towns; from the cultural inspiration of the Festival city to the moving experiences offered by the landscapes of the Flinders Ranges.

Looking across Elder Park towards the city.

The majesty of the Flinders Ranges.

Arts and Entertainment

Sport and Recreation

Business and Technology

Early Settlement

Just as people are shaped by their past, so too are places, and there is much in South Australia's heritage to explain the sense of *difference* which is part of its enduring charm. This was the first Australian colony to be founded free of 'convict stain' and financed by land sales. Those first white settlers who came to South Australia in 1836 were either landowners or labourers and expected to work hard and buy their own land as soon as possible. At the appropriate time self government would be granted. In this orderly way, it was proposed, a more stable and peaceful society would develop. So peaceful in fact, that in planning this utopia no provision was made for a police force. (As it turned out, the colony actually formed the first organized professional police force in Australia.)

B23516   *Native chief.*

The first vessel with emigrants arrived at Kangaroo Island in July 1836. Some hoped this would be the main settlement but along with other alternatives, including Encounter Bay and Port Lincoln, it was rejected by Colonel William Light in favour of the present site of Adelaide. On the 28 December 1836, Governor Hindmarsh arrived at Holdfast Bay and the proclamation was read. This lofty document enshrined freedom and justice for all and emphasised protection for the Aborigines with whom the inhabitants were expected to live in harmony. The settlers were called upon to conduct themselves with

'... order and quietness, duly to respect the laws, and by a course of industry and sobriety, by the practice of sound morality and a strict observance of the Ordinances of Religion, to prove themselves worthy to be Founders of a great and free Colony ...'

There was, however, neither order nor quietness in the arguments which ensued about Light's choice of capital. Governor Hindmarsh, in particular, did not approve of the site and the squabbles were a costly distraction for Light who was anxious to get on with his surveys. Light—the gallant soldier who had fought against Napoleon's forces in the Peninsula War—refused to back down and finally a meeting of landowners was held and a vote taken. Light's choice was confirmed 218 to 127.

Those first colonists were attracted by the high ideals espoused by Edward Gibbon Wakefield—the author of this new concept of *systematic colonisation*—and by the theorists who promoted the scheme. South Australia was most fortunate in the choice of Colonel Light as both Surveyor General and the man to choose the site of the capital and undertake the first surveys, city and

B10079 *Adelaide view. Sketch by Col. Light, of tents near the sight for the (then) proposed town of Adelaide.*

country. Light knew he held the future well-being and lifestyle of people in his hands. He was creating not just the administrative capital of a tiny Antipodean settlement, but a way of life. A future city, yes, but above all, a place for people. To the assignment he brought not only his skills as a surveyor, but also the characteristics of his former professions of soldier and sailor and his feelings as musician and artist. Ultimately his city plan with its squares, wide streets and parklands was practical and courageous, cultivated and visionary. Those lucky enough to call Adelaide home know that this gracious city is only now revealing the very deepest of its strengths as it faces with confidence the diverse challenges, human and structural, of the 21st century.

B43517   *Pioneer family and their slab hut at Naracoorte, 1890's.*

B47344 *Wallaroo mines, 1910.*

Colonel Light also demonstrated an awareness of his place in the history of South Australia when he concluded his *Brief Journal* with the oft-quoted words which are recorded on his statue overlooking the city on Montefiore Hill, North Adelaide '.....I leave it to posterity ..... to decide whether I am entitled to praise or to blame.'

The Adelaide site settled, the colonists left the on-going disputes to the officials as there were huts to be built, land to be worked and a living to be earned. Crude constructions on the River Torrens gave way to huts and houses and gradually imitation English villages dotted the landscape. However, the founder saw little of this development, for within three years of his arrival, Colonel William Light died as a victim of tuberculosis.

The inevitable growing pains of a city are felt most sharply in its roads and particularly in winter. These life-giving veins are essential for public transport and trade, but Adelaide's first roads were so bad stories abounded of animals perishing in the muddy depths. Growing districts became cut off from the city when bridges collapsed over swollen creeks in winter. The main artery from Adelaide to Mount Barker, via Glen Osmond and Stirling, was originally a track frequented by bushrangers and passing through private property. Eventually this track was developed into a major route from Glen Osmond. To cover the cost of the new road, South Australia's first and only turnpike gate was erected in the early 1840s at the bottom of Chimney Hill on Glen Osmond Road. Beside it was

B47385 *Wallaroo, Jetty and tall ships.*

built a hexagonal cottage —the toll house. Only the governor and church-goers could pass without paying tolls, but the system proved unworkable and the turnpike gate closed in 1847. The familiar toll house is now preserved as a reminder of an early example of public funding known today as 'user-pays'.

Up on the hill above the old toll house is a landmark of something which did pay; a remnant from the smelting works which was constructed in 1849 to smelt ores from the nearby silver-lead mine, worked from 1841-51. This was the first mining and smelting operation in Australia and Australia's first exports of ore came from here in 1843.

The following year Australia's first copper mine was opened at Kapunda. The timing was most fortuitous because the colony was in the throes of one of its many cash crises. It precipitated a great copper hunt during which a number of small finds caused brief flurries until the big one—Burra in 1845. The 'Monster' mine, as it became known, was to produce ore worth around five million pounds. The benefits from Burra and Kapunda flowed right throughout South Australia, creating fortunes for some and employment for others and an important increase in population.

B21701 North Terrace, 1910.

B39213 *Picnic, Tanunda.*

B8817 *Hahndorf, 1894.*

Mining again came to the aid of the colony's ailing finances in the 1860s. This time the discovery took place at Wallaroo, closely followed by another at Moonta. Port Wallaroo was set up with a smelting works connected by tram to Moonta and Kadina. These quickly became the biggest towns outside Adelaide and the copper triangle or 'Australia's Little Cornwall' was formed. The Moonta mine was the first in Australia to pay a million pounds in dividends and by the time it closed in 1923, it had earnt over twenty million pounds. The copper has gone but the traditions linger on in towns proud of their heritage and in festivals which cherish memories of the 'Cousin Jacks and Jennies'.

The discovery of copper was immensely important to the South Australian economy. A stroll along North Terrace, Adelaide's gracious 'boulevard of learning' reveals where some of the financial benefits of copper were spent. The University of Adelaide, the Elder Conservatorium, scholarships, chairs and schools of medicine and dentistry were endowed by two of the proprietors of the Wallaroo and Moonta copper mines— Sir Thomas Elder and Sir Walter Watson Hughes.

Perhaps the founder of the hills town of Hahndorf was a prophet. Back in November 1838, Pastor Kavel had led the first group of German settlers from oppression and economic uncertainty in their homeland to the new colony of South Australia. After a period at Klemzig on the outskirts of the capital, Kavel's congregation moved to the Barossa Valley where they founded Bethany and Tanunda. Kavel's arrival was followed soon after by Captain Dirk Hahn with more German settlers. On first seeing the land offered to him in the Mount Barker district, he declared 'nature had lavished her choicest gifts on South Australia'— and he was only talking about what he could see. The settlement was later named Hahndorf and in the 1840s, another band of Germans seeking religious freedom

arrived in the colony led by Pastor Fritzsche. Fritzsche later settled a number of families in a beautiful valley in the Adelaide hills—they named the location Lobethal ('Valley of Praise'). Here they farmed, brewed beer and began weaving. The famous Onkaparinga woollen mills began in an old brewery building at Lobethal. Sober and hard working, the Germans not only exemplified the theorists' desire for peace and stability, they changed forever the sights, sounds, traditions and even the aromas of the regions they settled. Church bells signalled times for work, meals, prayers and end of day and many travellers today are happily acquainted with the regional delights of German baking, beer drinking and sausage making which are major attractions at special festivals.

While copper was undoubtedly a big money earner for the colony, it couldn't be expected to last forever—not like the wheat and wool or the fruits of the vines which were flourishing in the Barossa Valley and the Southern Vales. In 1865, Surveyor General George Goyder drew an imaginary, cautionary line across the map of South Australia separating the areas suitable for agriculture from those more suited to pastoral use. A very talented and experienced surveyor who knew almost every inch of South Australia, his *line* would be ignored by some at great personal and financial cost. Optimistic farmers pushed further and further outward beyond Clare and on the Yorke Peninsula. Blyth, Booleroo Centre, Gladstone and Quorn became familiar to travellers. In the mid north many new towns were surveyed with layouts very similar to Adelaide; central business areas, surrounding parklands, then residential blocks and straight roads radiating out to the land beyond.

A decade later, a Yorke Peninsula farmer, Robert Smith, produced a very important piece of agricultural machinery—the stump jump plough. With the earlier Ridley Stripper, it was one of the most significant inventions in farming history and a shining example of the ingenuity of the South Australian farmer.

B17112   *Paddle steamer Pioneer, with barges carrying wool.*

B12381   *Tobacco leaf grown near Penola, 1932.*

As primary production increased, so did the demand for economical and efficient transport and thoughts turned to 'the River', the Murray. The river transport enthusiasts were passionate in their cause. In 1853, the colourful riverboat era was ushered in by a dramatic and very entertaining race between an adventurous Scot, Captain Francis Cadell and a Gumeracha flour miller, William Randell. The plan was to see who would be first to travel up the Murray and prove it was suitable for river trade.

For nearly half a century this river resounded with the swish and splash of paddles, the banter of the skippers and the laughter of the passengers. But ultimately the viability and romance of the riverboats could not withstand the impact of drought, roads, river taxes and the 'iron horse'.

The latter was to prove a vigorous and vital usurper, snaking out to service the expanding agricultural areas and leaving the Murray to do what it continues to do, irrigate the vineyards and orchards of the closely-knit settlements along its banks. Two Canadian brothers, George and William Chaffey came to Australia to help solve Victoria's water supply problems but thanks to some quick thinking by the South Australian premier of the day, the Chaffeys also selected river frontages in South Australia. In 1887, Renmark beat Mildura to become Australia's first irrigation colony.

Water has always bedevilled this driest of all the states. While inventions like the stump jump plough and the stripper and the provision of railways greatly expanded agricultural horizons, they still remained limited by a lack of water. When the railways reached Cummins and Kimba over on Eyre Peninsula, it became vital for Port Lincoln to establish a stable water supply. The building of tanks and reservoirs was only a temporary solution until the establishment in the 1920s of the Tod River scheme which supplied water to Port Lincoln and beyond to Thevenard.

Ironically, too much water hindered the development of parts of the South East —where heavy rainfall turned

B54098   Oyster men, Port Lincoln, 1909.

valuable grazing land into useless swamp. Again, the government turned to its brilliant surveyor-general, George Goyder. He devised a drainage system, taking a great personal interest in its construction. Very gradually another valuable area for agriculture, dairying and sheep breeding was settled and developed.

Wheat, wool, copper and wine—each played a dynamic role in the steady progression from colony to state. In the final analysis though, the worth of any human settlement is only the sum of its people. Their efforts largely undocumented except in what you see around you, it has been the ordinary men and women who have brought South Australia to the stable, contented community it is today. Their industry is evident in the physical structures and easy lifestyle and their ideals and tolerance are embodied in state laws.

There have always been great South Australian leaders in every field, but who do you single out for mention? Mawson for exploration, Florey for his role in the development of penicillin, Spence for social reform, Oliphant for science and so on? Perhaps, in this the Festival State you turn to a painter—to Sir Hans Heysen.

B15128 *Camel train at Blinman.*   B8338 *Walking race, 1903.*

B5468 *First electric tram, 1889.*

He taught South Australians to reach out with their hearts to the great gums and gorges of the Flinders Ranges and in so doing, open their minds to the bigger issues of conserving the natural beauty of the entire state.

As Colonel Light rightly knew, only posterity will judge the way in which future generations respond to challenges as vital as any faced by those idealistic colonists who turned an unknown wilderness into a pleasant place to live.

Adelaide

Adelaide is recognised as being one of Australia's most elegant and well planned cities. The city is bordered by quiet parklands and the easy-paced River Torrens flows through its heart. Many restaurants and cafes, some outdoor, offer a pleasant boulevard existence. The paved shopping area of Rundle Mall with its modern sculpture, seating and colourful flower and fruit stalls add to the relaxed atmosphere of the city.

The many art galleries and Festival Centre, (the focus of Adelaide's internationally recognised Festival of Arts), reflect the city's dedication to these areas of entertainment. Charming Victorian buildings, parklands and gardens offer many interesting walks. In the area of Elder Park, on the southern banks of the River Torrens, sits the Rotunda, a classic example of South Australia's elegant colonial architecture. For over a hundred years it has been a focal point of many celebrations and a delightful meeting place.

Lights Vision was originally built in 1906 as a dedication to the founder of the city, Colonel William Light. In 1938 it was relocated on the top of Montefiore Hill where it now points to spectacular views of the city and hills.

The excitement of Grand Prix racing in the heart of Adelaide.

The city of Adelaide is ringed with beautiful parklands.

The John Martins-State Bank Christmas Pageant.

The visual excitement of the Myer Centre, Adelaide.

The Festival Centre.

The Museum by night.

The climate encourages much outdoor life. In November, Adelaide hosts the international Grand Prix which is watched by large numbers of overseas visitors and local enthusiasts.

A special feature of Adelaide is its close proximity to so many fascinating regions. Lovely hills with their old-world towns and villages, pleasant wineries and wildlife parks are all within easy drives from the capital. The beaches along Gulf St Vincent are popular relaxation areas all year round. Of special importance are the famous coastline suburbs, Glenelg and Port Adelaide, which feature many interesting buildings and historical sites of early settlement.

The Rotunda was Sir Thomas Elder's gift to the city of Adelaide in 1881.

The tram ride from the city to Glenelg is a favourite jaunt for the tourist and an ideal way of seeing other suburbs.

Adelaide is the envy of other Australian cities. Variously called The Athens of the South, the Festival City and Grand Prix City, Adelaide offers a combination of excitement, relaxation and cultural stimulation.

Rundle Street. Outdoor restaurants are a feature of Adelaide's relaxed atmosphere.

Parliament House, North Terrace.

The fountain in Victoria square symbolises the three main rivers that supply the city with water.

North Terrace features much of Adelaide's architectural and cultural heritage.

A walk through the city will disclose many architectural gems: the University of Adelaide, Old Parliament House, Ayers House and Mortlock Library grace North Terrace; the many handsome cathedrals and churches, such as St Peter's Cathedral; and features such as the Torrens Rotunda, Victoria Square fountain and sculptural elements of the Botanic Gardens.

Established in the 1870's, the Adelaide Oval is one of the world's prettiest sporting venues.

A pleasant place to relax in the hub of the city.

Many ethnic backgrounds add colour to South Australian life.

The Shrine of Remembrance is situated on the corner of Kintore Avenue and North Terrace, near Government House. Unveiled in 1931, it is a splendid memorial to those who gave their lives in World War I. Statues on either side of the Shrine reveal a touching picture of community involvement during the war years.

Fitting words are carved into the Shrine: 'All Honour Give To Those Who Nobly Striving Nobly Fell That We Might Live.'

The Shrine of Remembrance.

The magnificent interior of St. Peter's Cathedral.

The Adelaide Himeji Gardens.

Interior of the Bicentennial Conservatory.

A thirty metre wisteria arbour, a stunning rose garden and an impressive avenue of Moreton Bay Figs form just a part of the internationally recognised Botanic Gardens. A tropical conservatorium, opened in 1989, houses an extraordinary collection of rare and common plants; many thousands of visitors pass through the gates every year to marvel at the magnificent rainforest environment.

The Botanic Gardens were officially opened in 1857. Forming part of the magnificent parklands that encircle the city, the eighteen hectare grounds offer a popular retreat for the garden loving population of the state.
A number of buildings, including the herbarium and the Palm House, are examples of classic Victorian architecture.

Containing nearly 4000 tropical plants the Bicentennial Conservatory is the largest in the southern hemisphere. Several medium sized trees and dense ground vegetation create a rainforest environment which can be clearly seen from two serpentine paths.

The tropical glasshouse is just one of a number of nineteenth century heritage buildings in the beautiful surroundings of the Botanic Gardens.

Memorial Drive, South Australia's tennis headquarters.

North Haven Marina.

The replica of the Buffalo now a permanent restaurant brings back memories of South Australia's earliest beginnings.

In 1878 the first horse-drawn trams made their appearance in the city. They could not exceed ten miles per hour through the streets and the drivers could be fined if they carried prostitutes. In 1908 the system was changed to electricity—this brought to an end thirty years of horse-drawn transport in the capital. This era will always be remembered with much affection.

Sunset at Glenelg jetty.

Adelaide Hills

The serenity of the Adelaide hills seems almost to mock the city onto which they look. From cottage industries, small inns and flour mills, the towns of Birdwood, Crafers and Stirling were formed. Though the mills and small industries have mostly disappeared, their buildings have passed into use as restaurants, galleries and quaint tea shops.

A scenic drive takes one through picture book villages set amongst private dwellings, small market gardens and farm buildings.

Though there has been much development through the years, the Adelaide hills still maintain an aspect of rural beauty and peace. The seasons are clearly marked—from the lovely blossoms in spring to the rich golds and reds of autumn. Large forests of natural vegetation cover much of the area. The more exotic European trees such as the oak and sycamore grow in abundance. Colonel Light was especially impressed by the beauty of the area and called it 'the Enchanted Hills'.

A typical small village set amongst the serenity and beauty of the Hills area.

Appletree Cottage

The Big Rocking Horse at Gumeracha, the tallest in the world at 18.3 metres high.

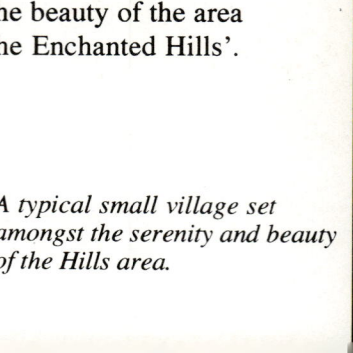

The annual Oakbank Easter Racing Carnival is one of the greatest holiday picnic race meetings in the world.

Motor Museum, Carrick Hill. A tourist alternative to the beautiful views of the Adelaide Hills.

The peaceful rural setting of the Adelaide Hills is only a few kilometres from the city.

Carrick Hill.

Kangaroos are only part of the wide variety of flora and fauna of the Cleland Conservation Park.

Small towns are rich in history and some like Hahndorf formed the beginning of European settlement in South Australia. The German heritage of this town is reflected in the architecture and Lutheran churches.

The hills are a unique part of South Australia's scenic beauty.

Wine Growing Regions

Containing some of the country's best known wine areas, these regions contribute to a special part of the South Australian lifestyle. With over 100 wineries and numerous award winning wines to their credit, these rich wine areas represent some of the best in Australia. Visitors can expect warm hospitality wherever they go. Wine tastings can be enjoyed in some of the most elegant and historic buildings in the state. The numerous restaurants offer many enticements to the food and wine lover. South Australia's wine regions have become Australia's largest wine producing areas.

The vines of the Southern Vales are amongst South Australia's oldest, the first being planted in 1838, two years after the founding of the colony. The region has a distinctive Australian atmosphere with some towns remaining almost as they were 120 years ago. The lovely towns of Clarendon, McLaren Vale and Reynella are favourite wine areas. The cellar of Chateau Reynella is considered the oldest still in use in Australia.

Just one of the many wineries of the valley.

Looking over part of the Barossa Valley.

Vintage Festival, Tanunda.

Barossa Valley's neat tapestry of fields and vineyards.

Barossa Valley's Balloon Regatta is a spectacular sight as dozens of balloons take to the skies.

Good music in pleasant surroundings.

A Lutheran church reflects the German past of the Barossa Valley.

The Barossa Valley, perhaps more famous than the Southern Vales, has a distinct German flavour. Old dwellings with thatched roofs and barns, the spires of Lutheran churches and large castle-like buildings reflect the traditions of the first German settlers. Barossa means 'hill of roses' and is the country's best known wine area. The wineries of the Barossa, though some are small, are mostly of grand architectural design. Pretty towns such as Angaston, Seppeltsfield and Tanunda have some of the most distinctive wineries of the region as well as containing historical sites and buildings of great heritage value to the state.

Vintage Festival.

30

Chateau Yaldara.

Herbig's Tree was the home of J.F. Herbig over 130 years ago.

Coonawarra Festival.

The beautiful Clare Valley has some twelve vineyards and forms one of the most vital wine communities of South Australia. Set in rolling, peaceful hills the friendly wineries offer wine tastings and informed comment on their prestige wines.

Festivals are a part of the celebrations of the wine year throughout the wine growing areas. The Barossa Valley's biannual vintage festival, with its ethnic dancing and merriment, attracts thousands of visitors from overseas and Australia. The Oktoberfest is also a popular event. Clare and McLaren Vale similarly hold their own wine festivals.

Coonawarra vines.

A cooper at work.

The special Barossa hospitality.

31

Fleurieu Peninsula

Nestled away in a small pocket south of Adelaide, the Fleurieu Peninsula presents some of South Australia's most contrasting scenery. Small rivers and creeks running off the Mount Lofty Ranges are a feature of the peninsula and, in Aboriginal legend, are thought to be the tears of the ancestral hero Tjilbruke. On the south coast daunting sea-beaten cliffs give way to deserted beaches.

Roads running through the rolling slopes of the Mount Lofty Ranges provide ever changing landscapes of beauty. Within an hour's drive from Adelaide is the prestigious wine producing area of McLaren Vale.

The quaint seaside towns of Victor Harbor and Port Elliot offer a relaxed atmosphere in a healthy climate. Goolwa, a charming river port, is famous for being the site of the country's first public railway in the 1850s.

Evidence still remains in much of the region of the old riverboat and sailing ship era.

One of several picturesque riverside parks in Strathalbyn.

Almond Blossom.

The horse tram from Victor Harbor to Granite Island.

McLaren Vale offers wine and food temptations in pleasant surroundings.

Steam Ranger.

Mouth of the Murray.

The Fleurieu Peninsula offers scope for the adventurous. Cliffs along parts of the coast present challenges to the experienced and beginner climber, while the southern end of the Heysen Trail is one of Australia's famous bush walks. For the nature lover, the Fleurieu Peninsula has twenty-one parks set in gentle hills and woodland.

The Riverland

A modern vessel captures the romance and adventure of the grand old days of the riverboat. They are a delightful way of seeing the River Murray landscapes.

The Riverland, known as the 'fruit basket' of South Australia, produces the state's major supply of oranges, apricots, peaches and pears. The riverside towns are prosperous and clean and offer a diversity of recreations. Fishing, canoeing and bushwalking are popular activities, while the gliding at Waikerie is considered to be the best in Australia.

Since the climate tends to be warmer here than in Adelaide, water occupies a great part of riverland life. Paddle steamers and modern houseboats are a common sight on the Murray River. The hiring of houseboats provides a delightful and relaxing holiday. More energetic water sports such as water skiing and power boat competitions are held regularly. Lake Bonney, at Barmera, offers fine sailing conditions.

Kookaburra.

A glider picks up the township of Waikerie with an equally stunning view of the orchards and vineyards bordering the River Murray.

Sunset reflected on the Murray.

Hairy nosed wombat.

Wineries present an increasing diversity to the region's economy. Some of Australia's largest and smallest wine producing areas are found here.

During the day magnificent pelicans fly above the riverside gums to find refuge further along the river. The area is also home to one of Australia's rarest animals—the hairy nosed wombat.

A pelican.

The spread of mallee and saltbush growth away from the irrigated areas present, in dramatic fashion, how human ingenuity can transform a desert into a productive region.

South East

Situated mid-way between Adelaide and Melbourne, the South East is a lush region within South Australia supporting large pastoral and timber industries. Together with the western district of Victoria, it is known as the Green Triangle. It was also the first named area of South Australia; Captain James Grant sailed along the coast in 1800 and called two extinct volcanoes after Admirals Gambier and Shank.

The landscapes of this region contain an incredible diversity. There are beautiful beaches and coastlines, while wetlands offer sanctuary for the numerous species of birds which breed in the area. This rich natural environment is preserved by thirty-two conservation parks and one national park.

The South East is famous for its seasonally inundated freshwater lagoons, lakes and swamps. Bool Lagoon is particularly noted for its extraordinary bird life. The Coorong is a major feature of the South East coastline and contains over 400 species of birds and a rich supply of fish. Fishing and boating are favourite pastimes in the area.

Sunset on the beautiful Coorong.

Mount Gambier's famous Blue Lake.

The Lady Nelson.

Padthaway House.

Robe Haven.

This area of South Australia has many geological wonders. Large caves formed by the weathering of limestone beds produce gigantic stalactites and stalagmites for which the area is famous. The limestone caves at Naracoorte and Tantanoola bring many people to the area. A unique feature of the South East is Mount Gambier's Blue Lake— its annual colour changes have confounded scientists for years. The Blue Lake is part of a vast volcanic plain that makes up an amazing array of lakes and parks.

Australia's largest concentrations of pinus radiata exist in the lower part of the South East. They form the basis of an important timber industry which includes about thirty sawmilling, woodchipping and cellulose plants.

Coonawarra's expanding vineyards and the fabulous crayfishing industries make the South East a popular food and wine region.

The South East contains numerous small and charming towns of which Robe and Penola are of special interest. Their old restored cottages and shops line the streets and provide a delightful hint of an earlier life.

Adam Lindsay Gordon wrote some of his best known verses in the South East.

The stalactites and stalagmites of the Naracoorte Caves. The caves are famous also for their extraordinary fossil discoveries.

Sinkhole diving in the Piccaninnie Ponds is an exhilarating and popular sport.

Yorke Peninsula

Originally composed of rich mining towns, Yorke Peninsula today is largely a cereal growing region. The old mining areas of Kadina, Wallaroo and Moonta, booming in the 1860s, now serve their purpose as valuable heritage areas of the state. Together these places became known as 'Little Cornwall' because of the vast Cornish influx during the mining boom. The Cornish heritage still lives on in the annual Kernewek Lowender Festival.

Quaint seaside towns sit on low cliffs descending to beaches which are usually quiet and deserted. The Yorke Peninsula is for people who enjoy such serenity. Fishing is a favourite pastime and the jetties at weekends are often crowded with people enjoying this activity.

A feature of the Yorke Peninsula is the lovely seasonal blooms of the wild lilacs and wattles. The Innes National Park offers spectacular coastal

Wheat harvests are a dominant landscape in the region. Nearly a third of the state's cereal crop is produced in the Yorke Peninsula.

Emus wandering in the beautiful Innes National Park.

Experience the pleasure of rural life with a farm holiday.

scenery with many secluded beaches. Some species of wildlife in the park such as the mallee fowl, western whipbird and southern pigmy possum are considered very rare. A network of roads gives easy access to all the towns of this beautiful peninsula.

The rugged coastline of Stenhouse Bay is a favourite caravan and bushcamping area.

A time to relax.

Eyre Peninsula

Taking in the western seaside town of Ceduna, encompassing Port Augusta to the east and all the lands to the south, the Eyre Peninsula is a vast track of land. Much of the area that John Eyre explored 140 years ago remains mallee scrub, though the dry inland that frustrated many of his plans is now a wheat and barley belt.

It is a flat land known for the beauty of its coastline on which pretty towns are situated. The wild extremes of the inland contrast with the sheer spectacular scenery of the coast from Tumby Bay to Coffin Bay. Boston Harbour on which sits Port Lincoln is considered one of the most beautiful natural harbours in the world. The area's two major national parks—Coffin Bay and Lincoln—are rugged and demanding. But the vast array of animal life including kangaroos, emus and numerous seabirds make them essential parks to visit.

Whales come to breed in the warm waters.

Tuna fishing is one of the large industries of the area.

40

Night view of Port Augusta Power Station.

Port Lincoln saw the early establishment of Lutheran and Anglican missions to help with Aborigines in the area. Whether missionary influence was of value or not, they did make a real effort to improve the situation of the Australian natives.

Part of the famous Lincoln Cove development.

Boston Bay at Port Lincoln featuring the 47m high silo complex.

Whyalla, the state's second largest city, stands on the east coast, its blast furnaces and mills producing large quantities of steel. Apart from this industrial complex, the Eyre Peninsula is mostly peace and beauty. Following the coastline down from Whyalla you come to Cowell, home of the world's largest black and green jade deposits.

With its mild climate, its many conservation parks and wide variety of water sports, Eyre Peninsula has always been a popular tourist resort.

Flinders Ranges

Some 450 kilometres north of Adelaide, the Flinders Ranges hold some of Australia's most spectacular scenery. The painters, Namatjira and Heysen, gave praise to the region in their famous works. Ridges and peaks thrust upward through wild, unspoilt terrain. Wildlife abounds and after rain wildflowers carpet the area in a breathtaking display.

Horse riding in the Flinders Ranges.

The geological history of the area holds particular fascination. The Flinders Ranges have their beginnings in sediment in the sea. Fossils found in their rocks date back to 600 million years ago. David Attenborough, during the production of *Life on Earth,* visited the area revealing the extraordinary fossilised remains. These were described as being amongst the first known forms of life.

The original granite and allied rocks which were later thrust upward by earth movements to form the ranges, date back as far as 1600 million years ago. This represents some of the most ancient landscape on earth. Later weathering and crustal movement gave shape to the remarkable mountain ranges. Over millions of years igneous rocks passing through complex geological processes have produced some of Australia's richest mineral deposits. Leigh Creek still mines large deposits of coal. The Flinders Ranges remain a rock hound's paradise with both rare and common stones found throughout the area.

Derelict towns and abandoned mine shafts are mute reminder of the area's once busy mining and pasture activity.

Rawnsley Bluff at morning.

Some picturesque views of the beautiful and serene Flinders Ranges.

Aboriginal Rock Painting.

Wilpena gum.

Rawnsley Park.

The Flinders is noted for its vegetation and wildlife. The state's floral emblem, the Sturt Desert Pea, is commonly found in the area. Magnificent river red gums are seen near creek and river beds. In the higher terrain, milder climates have allowed ancient ferns to grow. Salvation Jane, which has spread wild throughout the ranges, gives the area a brilliant colour in the spring. Animal life is abundant and varied. The giant red kangaroo, along with the emu and yellow footed wallaby can often be found on the plains. Galahs fill the area with their screeching, while birds of prey such as the nankeen kestrel hover gracefully in the sky.

Arkaroola.

The region also has an important Aboriginal heritage. The remains of Aboriginal rock paintings can still be seen in many places, including Arkaroo Rock on the eastern slopes of Wilpena Range and Sacred Canyon eighteen kilometres from Wilpena. Aboriginal legend has directly influenced the names of many places in the Flinders Ranges.

Pichi Richi Railway.

The extraordinary colours of the ranges and basin give the Flinders a sense of compelling mystery. Wilpena Pound is the Flinders' most famous point and from its peak the majestic beauty of the area can be seen.

The bush resorts of Wilpena Pound and Arkaroola are havens for the traveller after a day's bushwalking or rock climbing.

Kangaroo with joey.

Sturt Desert Pea. South Australia's floral emblem.

The Flinders Ranges is the gateway to outback Australia.

Mid North

The Mid North consists of an array of towns, farms, vineyards and mines and is one of the most interesting parts of the state. Its geographical boundaries take in the Clare Valley and northwards to Port Augusta, eastwards along the road to Peterborough and then west to the lovely fishing resort of Port Broughton.

From the stately homes of the Clare Valley, to the old cottages and quaint sandstone and bluestone dwellings around Burra and Jamestown, the Mid North boasts some of the state's most attractive buildings.

Much of South Australia's history is also focused in the area. The Burra copper mine saved the infant colony from bankruptcy in the 1840s. Pastoralists, attracted by the region's rich soils, took up huge runs that today produce the Merino wool that is internationally famous. Wineries have burgeoned throughout the lovely Clare Valley since the 1860s. It is

Bungaree, famous Merino parent stud property.

Kilkanoon Rest.

Burra Creek.

Geralka Farm where splendid Clysedales still plough the land in harness.

Martindale Hall, the 19th century Georgian mansion, is a favourite tourist visiting place.

little wonder that the area has been described as 'the land of milk and honey'.

The Mid North has successfully appeared on film. *Picnic at Hanging Rock* was filmed at Martindale Hall near Clare while the Burra Redruth Gaol was featured in *Breaker Morant*.

The inspiration for some of the poems of C. J. Dennis can be felt in his childhood home of Laura.

Burra Mines.

The Far North

North of the Flinders Ranges lies a world of harsh beauty, stony deserts, salt pans and sand hills. Known as the Far North and forming part of the outback region, it covers land many times the size of the world's largest cities and urban environments. Charles Sturt, while exploring this country in 1845, described it as having 'no parallel on this earth's surface'.

Towns are separated by many kilometres and their small populations respectfully observe the environment's harsh conditions. The history of the area has been one of pioneers and adventurous souls. Beneath wide skies and an eternal sun, the locals ply difficult occupations in mining and on vast cattle stations. The large gas fields at Moomba show up as a strange industrial silhouette on a flat, barren land.

Station owner.

There are three main deserts in the region. Sturt's Stony Desert in the north-east is a large area of stones or gibbers. The Simpson Desert, extending into South Australia from the Northern Territory and Queensland, consists of long parallel dunes of red sands. The Great Western Desert has been formed from the erosion of ancient rocks into plains of gibbers, salt pans and sand ridges.

Freak rain storms often transform the area into a natural sanctuary. Lakes forming in salt pans offer breeding grounds for native birds such as pelicans, ibis and herons.

The lonliness of the Sturt Desert.
Inset: Blue Tongued Lizard.

The Breakaways.

Lake Eyre.

Underground church.

Wildflowers, dormant through the long dry periods, burst in a spectacular display of colour. The outback's natural colours remain one of the area's most beautiful features. Vivid reds of deserts appear like fire while the crystal white of salt pans hurts the eyes with brilliant glare.

Because of the local conditions, travellers are warned to explore with caution. Following such advice, some of the world's most extraordinary landscapes can then be seen.

Andamooka cottage.

Kangaroo Island

Kangaroo Island is Australia's third largest island, located 100 kilometres south of the mainland coast. Four main towns—Kingscote, Parndana, American River and Penneshaw—support the island's sparse population. Its beautiful coastline with rugged cliffs and unspoilt beaches is met by restless seas throughout the year.

The placenames are a reminder of the island's diverse group of settlers and explorers. American River was established by an American whaling colony thirty years before the British landed on the mainland. Kangaroo Island was settled three months before ships arrived at Glenelg at the end of 1836. The French navigator, Baudin, explored the island in 1803 leaving romantic placenames such as Cape du Couedic, Cape Gantheaume and Distress Bay.

The spectacular scenery of Weirs Cove.

Island Navigator.

Conservation parks, including South Australia's largest national park—Flinders Chase—protect the abundant wildlife of the region. Kangaroo Island's special role as preserver of several animal species has made it something of a wilderness area in South Australia. In the 1920s the koala and platypus were introduced here to prevent their possible extinction on the mainland. Today the island has several koala colonies, while the platypus can be seen by the quiet and patient observer. South Australia's last remaining Glossy Black Cockatoos exist only on Kangaroo Island. Apart from these rarer species, animals such as the kangaroo, the unusual echidna and delightful little penguin can be commonly seen.

Christmas Cove.

Penguin.

Due to its isolation from the mainland, Kangaroo Island contains an extraordinary catalogue of animals and plant life. Approximately 750 native plants are thought to exist on the island. Flinders Chase has 443 of these alone, making it one of the most representative areas of natural vegetation in Australia. Commonly found species include a variety of gums, banksias, yaccas and she-oaks. However, some species like the beautiful Tekrathecas and the prickly Petrophila are found only on the island. In spring the island's many wattles burst with rich colour.

Australian sea lions.

Stalactites of Admirals Arch silhouetted by the sun.

All year round, the fascinating spectacle of flora and fauna, together with the beautiful coastline, give Kangaroo Island an impression of paradise.

SEASONAL GUIDE

SUMMER
Visit the beach.
Murray River cruises.
Water Skiing.
Sailing.
Visit Hahndorf for the Schutzenfest.
Go to Sky Show.
Go Fishing.

AUTUMN
Wine Tasting.
Visit the Zoo.
Hot Air Ballooning in the Barossa Valley.
Visit the Adelaide Festival of Arts and Fringe.
Visit the Botanic Gardens.
Visit a Wildlife Sanctuary.
Experience the Whispering Wall at Williamstown.
Visit the Oakbank Easter Racing Carnival.

WINTER
Whale watching off Victor Harbor.
Visit the Museum.
Visit Art Galleries.
Visit the Theatre.
Visit the Bicentennial Conservatorium.
Visit the Historic buildings of Adelaide.

SPRING
Bush Walking.
Wild Flowers in the Flinders Ranges.
Visit the Royal Adelaide Show.
Go to the Grand Prix.
See the Christmas Paegent.
Go on a picnic.
Travel the boardwalk at St. Kilda.

For more information on places to see and things to do, visit Tourism South Australia.